My False Teeth Fit Fine, But I Sure Miss My Mind!

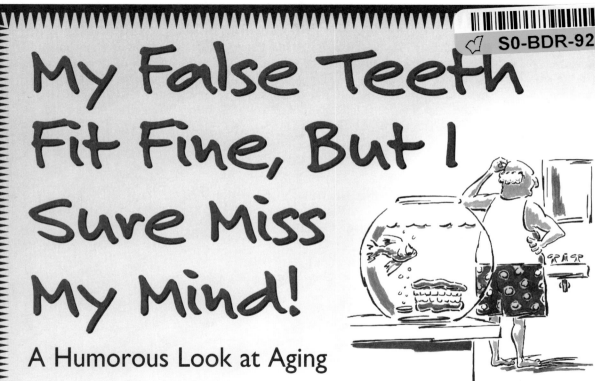

A Humorous Look at Aging

ISBN 1-889116-07-6

Printed in the United States of America

Second Printing

Design by
Paragon Communications Group, Inc., Tulsa, Oklahoma

Published by
PENBROOKE PUBLISHING
Tulsa, Oklahoma

My False Teeth Fit Fine, But I Sure Miss My Mind!

A Humorous Look at Aging

PENBROOKE
PUBLISHING

Tulsa, Oklahoma

One of the chief pleasures of
middle age is looking back at
all the people you didn't marry.
Anonymous

———— ◆ ————

I have everything now I had twenty
years ago—except now it's all lower.
Gypsy Rose Lee

You know you're getting older when the candles cost more than the cake.
Bob Hope

———◆———

Resolve to be tender with the young,
compassionate with the aged,
sympathetic with the striving,
and tolerant with the weak
and the wrong. Sometime in life
you will have been all of these.

Bob Goddard

You know you're getting old when you stop buying green bananas.
Lewis Grizzard

———— ⋅◆⋅ ————

As a person gets older, bingo becomes more and more fascinating.
Anonymous

Old age is like underwear;
it creeps up on you.
Lois L. Kaufman

———◆———

They say such nice things about
people at their funerals but
it makes me sad to realize that
I'm only going to miss mine
by just a few days.
Garrison Keillor

Be nice to your children because
they will choose your rest home.
Phyllis Diller

———— ⬩✦⬩ ————

An old man loved is winter with flowers.
German Proverb

Don't worry about becoming senile. You won't notice when it happens.

Anonymous

By the time you can read
a girl like a book,
your library card
has expired.

Milton Berle

————— ·•·•· —————

Middle age is when a narrow waist and a broad mind begin to change places.
Glenn Dorenbush

———◆◆◆———

Eat all you want and spend all your money because it's too late anyway and your kids don't really deserve it.

As long as you're over the hill
you might as well
enjoy the view.

Anonymous

———◆·◆———

If God had to give a woman wrinkles, He might at least have put them on the soles of her feet.

Anne de Lenclos

If I'd known I was going to live so long, I'd have taken better care of myself.

Eubie Blake

———•—•—

At 50 everyone has the face he deserves.

George Orwell

Middle age is when
your age starts to show
around your middle.

Bob Hope

Years ago we discovered the exact point, the dead center of middle age. It occurs when you are too young to take up golf and too old to rush up to the net.

Franklin P. Adams

When I was young,
the Dead Sea was still alive.
George Burns

———◆———

People who say you're just as old as
you feel are wrong, fortunately.
Russell Baker

How old would you be if
you didn't know
how old you were?

Satchel Page

One trouble with growing older is that it gets progressively harder to find a famous historical figure who didn't amount to much when he was your age.

Bill Vaughan

Pull out a gray hair and seven
will come to its funeral.
Pennsylvania Dutch Saying

———— •-•-◆-•-• ————

The old believe everything,
the middle-aged suspect everything,
the young know everything.
Oscar Wilde

Don't worry about tomorrow.
You never know what will
befall you today.

Yiddish Proverb

—•——◆——•—

I prefer to forget both pairs of glasses and pass my declining years saluting strange women and grandfather clocks.

Ogden Nash

If you survive long enough, you're revered—rather like an old building.

Katharine Hepburn

———◆———

Old age is no place for sissies.

Bette Davis

I'm at an age where my back goes out more than I do.

Phyllis Diller

I smoke cigars because
at my age if I don't
have something to hold on
to I might fall down.

George Burns

When you can finally afford the rings you want, you'd rather no one noticed your hands.
Lois Muehl

After a man passes 60, his mischief is mainly in his head.
Edgar Watson Howe

There's one advantage
to being 102—
no peer pressure.

Dennis Wolfberg

———◆◆———

If from life you take the best,
And if in life you keep the jest,
If love you hold;
No matter how the years go by,
No matter how the birthdays fly—
You are not old.

H. S. Fritsch

Crossing the street in New York keeps old people young—if they make it.

Andy Rooney

———— ·•· ————

Some people reach the age of 60 before others.

Lord Hood

Old age is when
candlelit tables are no
longer romantic because
you can't read the menu.
Lois L. Kaufman

From birth to age eighteen, a girl needs parents. From age eighteen to thirty-five, she needs good looks. From thirty-five to fifty-five, a woman needs personality. And from fifty-five on, the old lady needs cash.

Kathleen Norris

The years that a woman subtracts from her age are not lost. They are added to the ages of other women.
Diane De Poitiers

———◦◦◦———

The four B's of middle age: baldness, bridgework, bifocals and bunyons.
Anonymous

The older a man gets,
the farther he had to
walk to school as a boy.

Anonymous

———— ••◆•• ————

Middle age: when you're sitting at home on a Saturday night and the phone rings and you hope it isn't for you.

Ogden Nash

———— ❖ ————

A diplomat is a man who always remembers his wife's birthday but never remembers her age.
Robert Frost

———————◆———————

Old age is when all the girls look alike to you.
Mac Benoff

What [time] hath
scanted men in hair,
he hath given them in wit.

William Shakespeare

Life would be infinitely happier if we could only be born at the age of eighty and gradually approach eighteen.

Mark Twain

———•◦•———

Old age is when a person begins to exchange emotions for symptoms.
Anonymous

———— ·•·•· ————

We don't understand life any better at forty than at twenty, but we know it and admit it.
Jules Renard

Age will not
be defied.

Francis Bacon

———◆———

There are people who are beautiful in dilapidation, like old houses that were hideous when new.

Logan Pearsall Smith

Sixty is the age when one has spent twenty years in bed and over three years in eating.
Anonymous

——◆——

You don't stop laughing because you grow old; you grow old because you stop laughing.
Michael Pritchard

To me, old age is always
fifteen years older
than I am.

Bernard Baruch

The secret of staying young is to live honestly, eat slowly, and lie about your age.
Lucille Ball

———◆◆———

I am long on ideas but short on time. I
expect to live to be only about a hundred.
Thomas Edison

———————◆———————

Growing old is a bad habit which a busy
man has no time to form.
Andre Maurois

You're over the hill when elastic-waist pants seem appealing.

Anonymous

———◆◆———

Old age? That's the period of life when you buy a see-through nightgown and then remember you don't know anybody who can still see through one.

Bette Davis

Old age is when everything starts to wear out, fall out or spread out.
Anonymous

———⋄———

I am ready to meet my maker. Whether my maker is prepared for the ordeal of meeting me is another matter.
Winston Churchill

Retirement is a good opportunity to catch up on your reading and join a discussion group.

———— ❖ ❖ ————

You're aging when your actions creak louder than your words.

Milton Berle

Old age is the period of life when
a man begins to feel friendly
towards insurance agents.
Anonymous

———◆———

Young men think old men are fools; but
old men know young men are fools.
George Chapman

Youth is the gift of nature,
but age is a work of art.

Garson Kanin

———— ◆ ————

When grace is joined with wrinkles, it is adorable. There is an unspeakable dawn in happy old age.

Victor Hugo

One of the pleasures of middle age is finding out that one WAS right.
Ezra Pound

I never expected to have in my sixties the happiness that passed me by in my twenties.
C. S. Lewis

The years between fifty and seventy are the hardest.
You are always being asked to do things, and yet you are not decrepit enough to turn them down.
T. S. Eliot

Whenever a man's friends begin to compliment him about looking young, he may be sure that they think he is growing old.

Washington Irving

———◆———

The secret of life is enjoying
the passage of time.
James Taylor

———— •◆• ————

Age is something that doesn't matter
unless you're a cheese.
Billie Burke

You know you're getting old when you're sitting in a rocker and you can't get it started.

Milton Berle

Every time I try to take
out a new lease on life,
the landlord raises the rent.

Ashleigh Brilliant

———•◦•———

You have to BE an antique
to appreciate them.
Faye Madigan Lange

———— ◆·◆ ————

The only way to keep your health is to eat
what you don't want, drink what you don't
like, and do what you'd rather not.
Mark Twain

I have one thing in common
with my grandchildren—
we both get around
with a walker.

Anonymous

———•—•———

In the past few years I have made
a thrilling discovery. . .that until
one is over sixty one can never
really learn the secret of living.

Ellen Glasgow

All that one can do for the old is to shock them and keep them up to date.

George Bernard Shaw

———— ◆ ————

Forty is the old age of youth; fifty is the youth of old age.

French Proverb

Old age is a time
when exercise is more
important than ever.

———•—❖—•———

When a middle-aged man says
in a moment of weariness
that he's half dead,
he's telling the literal truth.

Elmer Davis

———◦•◦———

Old age is not so bad when
you consider the alternatives.
Maurice Chevalier

The greatest thing about getting older is that
you don't lose all the other ages you've been.
Anonymous

I adore my bifocals, my false teeth fit fine, my hairpiece looks good, but I sure miss my mind.

Anonymous

———◆◆◆———

Middle age is the time
a guy starts turning out lights
for economic rather than
romantic reasons.

John Marino

It's hard to be nostalgic when you can't remember anything.
Anonymous

Age merely shows us what children we remain.
Goethe

Old age is when you have
the same haircut as
your poodle.

Anonymous

———•◦◆◦•———

I'm sixty-five and I guess that puts me in with the geriatrics, but if there were fifteen months in every year, I'd only be forty-eight.

James Thurber

Just remember, once you're over the
hill, you begin to pick up speed.
Charles Schultz

———— ◆·◆·◆ ————

There's many a good tune played
by an old fiddle.
Proverb

My parents didn't want to
move to Florida,
but they turned sixty,
and it was the law.
Jerry Seinfeld

———◆———

I refuse to admit that I'm more than fifty-two even if that does make my sons illegitimate.

Lady Astor

———◆———

I am past thirty and three parts iced over.
Matthew Arnold

———◆———

Old men start giving good advice
when they can no longer
set a bad example.
Anonymous

Pay back time: Spoil your grandchildren rotten next time they visit. It will take their parents weeks to get them back to normal.

———— ◆◆ ————

You've reached old age when the gleam in your eye is just the sun on your bifocals.

Henny Youngman

Now that I'm over sixty, I'm veering towards respectability.
Shelley Winters

One starts to get young at the age of sixty.
Pablo Picasso

Middle age is when your wife tells you to pull in your stomach, and you already have.

Jack Berry

When I was younger I could remember anything, whether it happened or not.

Mark Twain

Old age has hit when you start pinching the cheeks of every child you meet.
Anonymous

The principal objection to old age is that there's no future in it.
Anonymous

Nobody loves life
like an old man.

Sophocles

———••◆••———

"Your teeth are like stars," he said,
and pressed her hand so white.
He spoke the truth,
for like the stars,
her teeth came out at night.

Anonymous

———◆———

Last Will and Testament: Being of sound mind, I spent all my money.
Anonymous

Old age is to be out of war, out of debt. . .out of the dentist's hands.
Ralph Waldo Emerson

After thirty, a body has
a mind of its own.
Bette Midler

Old people shouldn't eat
health foods.
They need all the
preservatives they can get.

Robert Orben

———◆———

The first sign of old age: it is when you go out into the street. . .and realize for the first time how young the policemen look.
Seymour Hicks

———◆◆◆———

Middle-age is when the best exercise is discretion.
Laurence J. Peter

Now that I can afford
a big house, I don't have the
energy to clean it.

Denise Tiffany

❖

It's a sign of old age when you feel like the day after the night before and you haven't been anywhere.

Anonymous

———•◦•———

Old age is alot of crossed off names
in an address book.
Ronald Blythe

———————◆———————

You have reached old age when you no
longer care where your wife goes,
providing you don't have to go along.
Anonymous

Other Penbrooke Books You Will Enjoy:

Love Letters To Remember (ISBN # 1-889116-02-5)
Letters to Mother (ISBN # 1-889116-00-9)
Everlasting Friendship (ISBN # 1-889116-04-1)
Sister Of Mine (ISBN # 1-889116-08-4)
Significant Acts of Kindness (ISBN # 1-889116-01-7)
The Little Book of Happies (ISBN # 1-889116-03-3)
A Timeless Gift of Love (ISBN # 1-889116-05-X)

To order additional copies of this book, or any of our other books,
call toll-free 1-888-493-2665

Do you have a humorous quote about aging?
We'd like to know. Write us at:

PENBROOKE PUBLISHING
P.O. Box 700566
Tulsa, OK 74170

PENBROOKE

PUBLISHING

P.O. Box 700566
Tulsa, OK 74170